WISDOM OF AGE

Sage advice from individuals
on the threshold of life's adventure,
those on the pathway to self-discovery,
and others looking back.

Jeff Rubin

Illustrations by Tanya Stewart

Copyright © 2019 by Jeff Rubin

jeff@wisdomofage.net

502-353-0255

All rights reserved. No part of this book may be reproduced in any manner without permission of the author, except in the case of quotes used in critical articles and reviews.

Cover design: Tanya Stewart

Text layout & design: Rubin-Hagan Assoc.

ISBN: 978-1-7337718-1-8

This book was produced by:

One World Press
890 Staley Lane
Chino Valley, AZ 86323
928-848-6550

printmybook@oneworldpress.com

www.oneworldpress.com

In Memory

In memory of Dr. Everett William Schaeffer (1917-2015), an inspiration and role model to everyone fortunate enough to have known him. "Doc," as he was affectionately called, passed away peacefully at the ripe old age of 98. Vibrant, exuberant, and caring throughout his life, he remained active, committed, and involved in the welfare of others literally right up until his death. This exceptional, yet humble human being had a zest for life that defied and defined his years. A "change agent" long before the term was coined, he epitomized the difference that one human being and one person's life can make.

He was representative, too, of every older person who believes that the elixir of life lies less in how others may view one's advancing years and more in how we view ourselves.

Insights from Readers

"I loved reading it. I loved the variety of ages and the complexity of answers in such brief statements. I was enamored by the depth of students' comments at such early ages (some six and seven-year-olds, along with several 13 and 14-year-olds really blew me away with their maturity!). I could see this as someone's personal favorite."

Elmer Thomas, Superintendent
Madison County Schools

"This book can be a powerful witness to our perceptions and misperceptions of the aging process. The variety of opinions give a lot to chew on and think through. The testimony from children and adults gives the matter depth. The book is a 30-minute read, but could be a several months' journey."

Rabbi Marc Aaron Kline, J.D.
Monmouth Reform Temple

"This compendium of wisdom is local and immediate. Rubin's work reveals that peace-of-heart and meaning are something everyone around us searches for, and the paths they have found are ones we can walk too. All we need to do is listen."

Chris Green, Director
Loyal Jones Appalachian Center
Berea College

"Rubin has captured in this work a glimpse at the threads of wisdom that weave the fabric of our lives – snippets, emotions, and insights from across the spectrum of ages that make up our collective human experience. Many will benefit from reading it; most who do will likely share it with others."

Keith R. Knapp, PhD, CNHA, CNA
Associate Professor/Chair
Dept. of Health Services/Senior Living Leadership
Bellarmine University

"This is a fine book that speaks to what we both are trying to accomplish, i.e. to get people to believe in themselves, ignite their passion, and discover their purpose. *Wisdom of Age* shows that we are both teachers and learners throughout our lives. The children in this book teach us that you don't have to live many years to be wise. The elders and youngsters show each other how common values and habits are important for all of us, lifelong."

Jan Hively, PhD
Encore Entrepreneur

Foreword

This book is dedicated to the fight against ageism and the misperception that one number or any number should define an individual's value and self-worth or exclude them from remaining active, relevant, and engaged. It presumes, instead, that anyone can think, dream, and influence the world around them regardless of their ability or age.

When introducing you to the wisdom you will find inside, it is important to first put the term "old" into perspective. There is no set definition or general agreement on the age at which a person becomes old. Various dictionaries have defined it in different ways. Some refer to it as "having lived for many years" or showing "characteristics of age." Others see it as being "experienced" (gaining skills and knowledge from experience), "worn" (like old shoes), "discarded" (no longer in use), and even "tiresome" (gets old fast).

The search for a definition is said to date back as far as 1875 in Britain, when the Friendly Societies Act (like

AARP now), defined old age as, "any age after 50." Over the years (thank goodness) that definition has evolved to reflect to some extent our increasing longevity and changes in the workplace.

Most people today use statutory or occupational retirement, usually between the ages of 60 and 65, to define the beginnings of aging. However, when we speak in terms of "retirement" we must now consider three generations of "old." They are generally defined as: the GI Generation, those born between 1901-1926; the Mature or Silent Generation, those born between 1927-1945; and Baby Boomers, those born between 1946-1964.

The United Nations has refused to adopt a standard criterion for aging. This may be attributed to the fact that while most developed countries use chronological time to define "old age," many parts of the developing world considered chronological years to have little or no significance. Instead, old age was defined more by the culture of each society and the roles they assigned or continue to assign to older people. In some cases, it is the loss of these roles due to physical decline that is considered the significant factor. In such an environment, old age is seen to begin at the point when active contribution is no longer possible. Active contribution is more than just the ability to remain physically active or to participate in the labor force.

It further includes continuing to contribute in social, economic, cultural, spiritual and civic affairs, and applies to both individuals and population groups.

"Active aging" is used to describe the shift in thinking taking place in many circles and communities today. It is used along with terms like "aging in place", "livable communities", "communities for all ages", and similar descriptions to explain a proactive approach to planning for and taking care of ourselves and others as we age.

Each presumes that aging is a continuum where people of all ages are afforded the opportunity to realize their potential for physical, social, spiritual, and mental well-being throughout their lives. There society provides them with adequate protection, security, and care when needed. It further provides an environment where people who retire from work, are ill, or live with disabilities can remain active contributors to their families, peers, communities, and nations.

This book is intended to expose the reader to the wisdom available to us all along life's continuum and to see the world through the eye of the beholder.

Within these pages expect to find the hopes, fears, doubts, regrets, dreams, inspiration, and sage advice from people on the threshold of their life's adventure, as well as those looking back on the paths already taken.

WISDOM OF AGE

Lastly, the advice given within is not intended to be read from cover to cover. Instead, I would encourage you to begin on any page. Thumb through it and dog ear it wherever you like. Give yourself the time to ponder, reflect, and revisit all that lies within. Whatever your age, expect to find the type of encouragement, comfort or advice that can only be found through experience and the wisdom that comes with age.

Jeff Rubin, Author

06/28/51

Contents

■	Acceptance, Faith and Attitude	Page 1
■	Kindness, Caring and Empathy	Page 13
■	Insight/Hindsight	Page 21
■	Regrets/Mistakes/Changes	Page 31
■	Health and Wellness	Page 39
■	Living in the Moment	Page 43
■	Relationships	Page 49
■	Respect/Age	Page 55
■	Encouragement	Page 61
■	Perceptions, Realities and Numbers	Page 66
■	Ageism: The Elephant in the Room	Page 86
	Postscript	Page 93
	The Wisdom of Age Survey	Page 94
	One Final Thought	Page 98
	Special Thanks	Page 99
	About the Author	Page 103

xiii

Acceptance, Faith and Attitude

"None of us are guaranteed a day with people we love. We are blessed with every day that we get up. Truly each is a gift. If we waste the time that we have getting angry or upset, we waste the gift. Life is too short to waste this gift."

Marc, Age 56
Rabbi

WISDOM OF AGE

If you could share one thing about life (that you've learned so far) with someone younger than you, what would that advice be?

"Life is about being happy, loving, and caring."

Caleb, Age 9

"Always have positive thoughts and you will have a great day."

Summer, Age 8 ¾

"Try to be positive even in a negative situation."

Melody, Age 13

"Don't worry about the little things in life because when you're older or even in a little time it probably isn't going to matter anyway."

Mary, Age 14

"Be the positive influence that someone else may need."

Louise, Age 43
library media specialist

Acceptance, Faith and Attitude

"Look for joy in every circumstance. Even when things are difficult or bleak, find the 'silver lining' in every situation. It may be something very small, or not easy to find. It may even be the opportunity to learn that you don't want to repeat that particular experience or situation. By maintaining a grateful attitude, all circumstances of life seem more pleasant and the difficult ones more bearable."

Tim, Age 63
communications

"Live life to the fullest and help others even if you are having a bad day. Choose your own weather. Don't let anyone get you down and remember if you are having a bad day there is always someone else having a bad day too so you are not alone."

Abby, Age 10

"Live life to the fullest. It's the only one you have so have fun, try things, but think and make sure it won't kill you. So, do as much as possible and live as long as you can."

Jacob, Age 18

Don't get bored more than once a month."

Aiden, Age 11

"If you're scared of something just do it. We are both young and we can do more than older people. Just don't think about it and you won't be scared."

Kayley, Age 10

"Pray every day of your life. (I do.) Live a long and healthy life."

Isaac, Age 11

"Put God first and spend all the time you can with your loved ones because life is short at best!"

**Stephen, Age 32
home care giver**

Acceptance, Faith and Attitude

Ageing is as much about a state of mind as it is the state of the body. If you start each day with a sense of awe about the world you are privileged to live in (and to praise God for it), and renew your commitment to make the most of that day--to care for yourself, your family and others, to learn, to experience, to share, to laugh, and don't go to bed too early--you are living well no matter what the numerical state of your age."

Dave, Age 63
newspaper publisher

Acceptance, Faith and Attitude

"Get up every day go to work, enjoy life, help others and let God direct your life."

Catherine, Age 90

"Be thankful, love the lord and others. Be cheerful."

Charlotte, Age 98

"Take time to be young and don't want to be grown up because if you're grown up you can have less time to do your favorite things."

Ella, Age 11

"Never work too hard."

Erica, Age 10

"Don't stress yourself out too much; its ok to have a day off."

Aly, Age 16

"Don't stress over the things you can't control. Everything works out in the end, and if things aren't worked out, it is not the end."

Kaelyn, Age 17

"Don't worry so much; it usually works out in the end."

Beth, Age 34
licensed psychological practitioner

WISDOM OF AGE

"Don't sweat the small stuff. Everything, even the most painful, difficult situations, will eventually pass. Invest in people, they're the most important 'things' in our life. And finally, . . . It's never too late to start over."

David, Age 41
pastor/missionary

"Take time to be still and listen to your own inner Spirit."

Peggy, 58
coach

"Don't let unimportant things weigh you down."

Janet, Age 71
teacher

"Take life one day at a time."

Hugh, Age 90

"Take it easy."

Aida, Age 93

Acceptance, Faith and Attitude

"Calm down; don't take yourself so seriously; you didn't get where you are solely on your giftedness; you got there because a lot of people helped you out. As the airline adage says: 'Put your own mask on first before helping others', but by all means, help others grow."

Sylvia, Age 66
attorney/leadership coach/consultant

"Find your passion, some would say your calling--something at which you are very good--and pursue it relentlessly. Take time to create a personal mission statement."

Guy, Age 59
nonprofit executive/philanthropy expert

"Do what you love and don't feel guilty or ashamed about being who you are."

Nancy, Age 69
housewife

"Do what you love-- follow your bliss."

Dennis, Age 71
leadership development coach

"Find your center. Seek balance and equanimity."

Garth, Age 74
ministry

WISDOM OF AGE

"No matter what age you are always remember your 'Divine Inner Child' helping you to stay connected to the transcendent! Seek out the wisdom of the elders, especially when times are uncertain for you, and find a trustworthy guide. No matter what, live as lovingly and joyfully as you are able to."

Magdalena, Age 66 and 1/2
clinical therapist

"We don't stop playing because we get old; we get old because we stop playing."

Gary, Age 62
advocacy/senior issues

"Surround yourself with younger people and you will always feel younger."

🙂 **Louise, Age 43**
teacher

"Age is only a number. Some young people are old and some old people are very young."

Gladys, 63
RN - case manager

Acceptance, Faith and Attitude

"*Old age is a state of mind. It is attitude! You can be old at any age It is just a number. Enjoy each day that you are blessed to have here on earth.*"

Carol, Age 71
secretary

Kindness, Caring and Empathy

"Decide what will make you truly happy (in your career, relationship, etc.) and fight/strive/work every day to get there because life is composed of lots of days--that's lots of mornings when you'll need to wake up knowing that the slog ahead of you is worthwhile, and lots of nights when you'll need to put your head on the pillow and know in your heart that you're still moving (however slowly) in the right direction."

Lorne, Age 34
composer, conductor, artistic director

WISDOM OF AGE

If you could share one thing about life (that you've learned so far) with someone younger than you, what would that advice be?

"Try your hardest and do your best."

Aubrey, Age 7

"Don't give up at something you are good at."

Jayden, Age 10

"Don't give up on something you love."

Bryce, Age 12

"Follow your dream and not someone else's."

Taryn, Age 9

"Don't let anyone disrespect you."

Cade, Age 10

"Always believe in yourself because if you don't then you don't know what you are capable of doing in life (like wonderful things)."

Morgan, Age 12

Kindness, Caring and Empathy

"Life gets hard but you will get through it. You will make new friends and create a new chapter of life!"

☺ ***Kayleigh, Age 9***

"Always be yourself."

Briana, Age 10

"If I could share one thing that I've learned so far it would be to say never, ever give up because eventually you will reach your goal and I would tell this to my little sisters."

Michelle, Age 11

"Life is full of adventures. Live life to the fullest. Don't sit around all day watching TV. Take time to enjoy life."

Reagan, Age 12

"Enjoy being young and learn from your mistakes. Never give up. Set a goal high and don't stop till you get there."

Damion, Age 11

"Whatever you want to do in life, go for it even if anyone thinks you can't. Just remember God is on your side!"

Jaylen, Age 13

WISDOM OF AGE

"You are beautiful and handsome no matter what anybody else may say. Just because of your age doesn't mean you can't make a change in the world. Love yourself and always know you are special."

Sophia, Age 9

Kindness, Caring and Empathy

"Make the most of every opportunity you are given. Don't be afraid to push yourself. Try to become the best possible version of yourself, but do not give in to others' demands of who you should be."

Tyler, Age 21

"Don't let people or fear hold you back."

Taylor, Age 22

"Don't let fear stop you, because if you do, then it will be one of the biggest regrets of your life."

Zack, Age 24

"If I could give one piece of advice I would say don't give up. My sister got in a huge cheerleading accident and almost died. She still can't talk because she got hit in the throat but this incident has made her very strong and I look up to her. She has been in 33 surgeries and she is so brave."

Ella, Age 13

"Never settle with Good Enough. I want to be a pilot. Once a pilot said to me, 'Never settle with Good Enough. Don't settle for 100 ft. lower or higher. Give it the best you can. Settle for the best of all.' You can accomplish anything as long as you don't settle with Good Enough."

Sara, Age 20

WISDOM OF AGE

"Just keep going with what life throws at you."

Tory, Age 10

"Don't hide behind a mask because you are embarrassed. Don't care what people think. You are special just the way you are."

Taylor, Age 10

"Enjoy being young and learn from your mistakes. Never give up. Set a goal high and don't stop till you get there."

Damian, Age 11

"Don't let what other people think stop you from doing something that would make you happy."

**Riley, Age 22
college student**

"Be true to yourself and don't try to be something you're not."

**Andy, Age 63
radio broadcasting**

Kindness, Caring and Empathy

"Follow your dreams no matter what someone else says. You're never too young or too old to make your dreams come true. If someone laughs at your dream, go home, have a good cry, then go somewhere else. It might not be easy, but keep trying. With hard work and God's help, nothing is beyond your dreams. Only you can destroy your dream."

Pat, Age 77
homemaker, caregiver, author

"We are both teachers and learners lifelong. Live your learning."

Jan, Age 85
educator/entrepreneur

Insight/Hindsight

"Experience is our greatest teacher, and we gain the experience of a lifetime in our living. There are those who have gained a head start on us in terms of our birth years, and the others of us who have a similar head start on the younger generations. Yet, we are all connected and can learn deeply from one another. I learned this lesson at age 22 when a six-year old helped me understand that, in her eyes, I was 'old.' Age is relative to the lens of the viewer or doesn't have to exist at all in terms of how we see, value, and appreciate life and the diversity of the ages."

Robert, Age 61
CEO

"Learn how to count to 100."

Aidan, Age 5

Insight/Hindsight

If you could share one thing about life (that you've learned so far) with someone younger than you, what would that advice be?

"I would tell them that life is hard."

Beanna, Age 7

"Learn how to log on to PBS Kids."

Byson, Age 5

"Learn your colors."

Meghan, Age 6

"Learn how to read!"

Zack, Age 5

"Be prepared for hard math questions."

Noah, Age 5

"I would tell them that an 'e' at the end of a word makes the vowel say its name."

Elliot, Age 5

"Never brag about your dog."

Bella, Age 7

WISDOM OF AGE

"Know where your classroom is."

Skye, Age 5

"When a teacher is talking, you should listen because it could be useful later in life; for example forty-two plus fifty-five you could use expanded form."

Braden, Age 8

"Life is hard but you get good moments."

Keaton, Age 8 and a half

"Life is not always easy. Always try hard and usually something good will happen."

Katie, Age 10

"While not always fair, life is very rewarding."

Alan, Age 65
consultant

"I would tell them about the 7 habits (of successful people)."

Vandre, Age 7

"Life is too valuable to throw away."

Katlyn, Age 14

Insight/Hindsight

"One life lesson that I have learned is that life moves on. You may be part of a drama one day but in the next day no one will care."

Landon, Age 14

"Something I have learned about life is never lie. If you are honest the first time you won't get in as much trouble as if you had lied. That is my advice as a life lesson."

Rachael, Age 10

"Never stop growing and learning, never stop examining yourself and your assumptions, help other people, live up to your word, make time for things that matter, and try to understand what compassion is and make it the basis for your life."

Peter, Age 61
non-profit administrator

"Stay in school and don't do drugs."

Emily, Age 12 ½

"Don't drink, don't do drugs, don't drive your parents' truck into a tree." (P.S. I did not learn this from experience.)

Evan, Age 12

"Do your homework even though you don't want to."

Isabella, Age 11

WISDOM OF AGE

"Plan early, give yourself time to think about your future, but don't take too long. Always be one step ahead."

Rhea, Age 21
college student

"Do well in high school so you can get into a good college. Education is important."

Alexandria, Age 21
college student

"Believe that every day is a gift. Be happy and enjoy every minute of it."

Mark, Age 44
estimator/contractor

"Travel more, own less, and practice gratitude every day."

Jackie Age 42
animal behaviorist

"Release all things that clutter your life. This includes negativity and judgement. It also includes physical items that make life more difficult by requiring maintenance. Time is your most important resource."

Patricia, Age 68
social worker/therapist

Insight/Hindsight

"Set goals for your life. Follow through whatever it takes to reach these goals. Be patient – if it takes you longer than you expect, the reaching of the goals will be worth it."

Paulette, Age 73
retired teacher

"Trust the process, and know it will always work out."

Donna, Age 59
psychotherapist

"Live life to your fullest. Do things. See things. Treat folks as you would like to be treated. Take notes and pictures about all people, places, and doings while it is available. It will be very interesting to you later as time goes fleeting by. Life lasts much longer than you think when you are a young adult. You will likely have multiple careers and many, many friends and acquaintances. Over the decades, you will experience great changes in culture and everything about your life's context. Never stop reading and caring."

Lyle, Age 62
administrator, higher education

"Life is short."

Bob, Age 87

WISDOM OF AGE

"Life goes fast, so work hard but take time 'to smell the roses.' Love your family and your children and take time for them."

**Edwin and Sylvia, Ages 83 and 80
counselor, minister/teacher**

"Be considerate of others and others' feelings and treat them as you would want them to treat you. Put on a happy face even if you aren't feeling very happy because no one likes a sour puss. Be honest and true because you are judged by others and someday by G-d himself."

Shirley, Age 95

Insight/Hindsight

"Life is too short to be worried about the number on your driver's license or the number on the scale."

**Candace, Age 45
strategy director, aging in community**

Regrets/Mistakes/Changes

"Life is making adjustments."
Hannah, Age 94

WISDOM OF AGE

If you could share one thing about life (that you've learned so far) with someone younger than you, what would that advice be?

"Sometimes there will be disappointments in life."

Elliott, Age 7

You will make mistakes in your life. Like me, I make mistakes. Grownups make mistakes. So, if you make a mistake, don't cry, don't feel bad because that's how life is.

Ava, Age 8

"Don't get stuck on the sad things in life."

Conner, Age 9

"If I was to share something about life that I've learned so far it would be that everyone makes mistakes."

Marissa, Age 10

"Sometimes things don't go the way you planned but better things can happen because of it."

Elaina, Age 13

"Learn from your mess ups."

Derek, Age 16

Regrets/Mistakes/Changes

"Learn from your mistakes."

Marguerite, Age 89

"I would tell them they should think before they do something because I have done things that I regret and I wish that I could go back and undo them. So make sure you think before you do something."

Gabi, Age 13

"Try not to make major decisions before you're 25 (i.e. marriage, babies, and tats.)"

Carrie, Age 71

"Only regret the chances you didn't take. Life is about adventure."

Kenzie, Age 14

"Twenty years from now you will be more disappointed by the things that you did not do than by the ones you did." – Mark Twain

Ki-Wan, Age 40
college professor

"You make your own destiny. Don't be afraid to take risks."

Nicholas and Shelby, Ages 17 and 16

"Keep trying new things and take on new responsibilities."

Phyllis, Age 72
RN, MSW

Be kind to yourself. I once thought my younger body was too dimpled and fat... And then one day I got pregnant and had children and my body really got dimpled and fat. My old body was lovely and I never loved it. I have learned to love this newer aging shell I am and I am so much happier for it. I wish I hadn't wasted so much energy on self-hate."

Amanda, Age 39
librarian

"Mistakes are inevitable. You always have a chance to learn from those mistakes. Your identity and worth don't have anything to do with your mistakes. Continue to grow. Keep an open mind. Life almost never works out like you plan it, so don't get stuck when it flips the script."

Alexys, Age 21
college student

Regrets/Mistakes/Changes

"*Everything always changes; the good and the difficult. Just trust the universe and do your part to be the best person you can be at the time.*"

Harriette, Age 70
CEO, not-for profit

"*There is no right or wrong way of doing things in life and in general, what you do is going to have to be done your own way. Nobody ever lives long enough to make all the mistakes that are possible in life. It doesn't hurt to learn from mistakes of others and to better understand what people have done before. So look for things that can be taken and adapted and used to improve your own circumstances and chances of success. Ask lots of questions – and question everything.*"

Mike, Age 49
director of social enterprises

"*Make choices that help you grow.*"

Janet, Age 73

Always pay yourself first."

Keith, Age 92

WISDOM OF AGE

"We were always going to take our honeymoon in Switzerland when we had money saved up. My wish now is we should have borrowed the money and gone on. We would have gotten it paid back and had our memory of a life time. But my husband became ill at 50 years of age and passed on."

Mary, Age 92 years and 2 months

"One of the most important life challenges is learning to let go, which allows us to change and grow and become more and more of who we are and can be. I would share with them the prayer by Dag Hammarskjold: "For all that has been Thanks. To all that will be, Yes."

Theresa, Age 71
minister, teacher, writer

Regrets/Mistakes/Changes

"I would tell them to remain curious and not be afraid to get out of their comfort zone. Comfort zone preserves the status quo. Comfort zone develops fear of risk taking. Playing it safe means that you are standing still as the world progresses. One of my favorite quotes (attributed to a woman named Jessie Potter): 'If you always do what you have always done, you will always get what you have always gotten'; truly sums up this sentiment."

Alex, Age 63
college professor

"When you intend to walk through a mine field, follow someone. Good decisions come from wisdom. Wisdom comes from making mistakes. Wisdom from other people's mistakes is the least costly."

Charles, Age 64
real estate appraiser

"Stay Active and Interested
in people around you.
Don't let a few aches and pains hold you back.
As you age your world becomes smaller.
It takes energy and motivation
to maintain your place."

Doris, Age 83

Health and Wellness

"Getting older is just another stage of life. Prepare for your age. Take care of your body and mind. Exercise, eat right, continue learning, and stay involved in activities that you enjoy every day."

Mary, Age 52
counselor

WISDOM OF AGE

If you could share one thing about life (that you've learned so far) with someone younger than you, what would that advice be?

"Don't watch too much TV."

Desire, Age 8

"My mama said early to bed, early to rise keeps you healthy, wealthy, and wise."

Kinsley, Age 9

"Drink lots of water."

Ashlyn, Age 10

"Pain is weakness leaving the body. That should give you hope and courage."

Anne, Age 8

"The phrase 'use it or lose it' is not just a phrase. Whether it is walking or talking or playing or interacting with other people. Once you stop doing it, you can't start again."

Yvonne, Age 59
bookkeeper

Health and Wellness

"Do all you can to take care of your health. Eat wisely and keep moving. Meet people and value relationships. Find someone who genuinely makes you happy."

Robert, Age 67
minister/teacher

"Keep active, have hobbies, be a volunteer, eat well, be part of friendship groups."

Frank, Age 70
director, non-profit, social work

"You need to get a good night's sleep, exercise, and plenty of fresh air."

Ophelia, Age 83

"Enjoy life while you are physically and mentally able."

Carolyn, Age 85

"I would advise people to do recreational exercise, stay active, keep their mind busy, and travel a lot."

Shirley, Age 86
retired school teacher

"Exercise (walk, walk, walk), practice good eating habits (I have cut out starches), laugh regularly, enjoy gardening."

Judith, Age 91
retired physician

"Slow down, you have the rest of your life to be an adult. When you're young, you don't really grasp the fact that youth is temporary because that's all you've known, but as you get older you realize just how short a period of time youth is when compared to a lifetime."

Rosalyn, Age 19

student

Living in the Moment

"Take the time and focus to learn about yourself and what gives you joy. Try to be present in the moment, and take praise and blame equally inconsequentially"

Ruth, Age 68
retired technical writer and trainer

WISDOM OF AGE

If you could share one thing about life (that you've learned so far) with someone younger than you, what would that advice be?

"Don't go faster than the speed limit."

Anderson, Age 6

"Try to be a kid as long as you can."

Landon, Age 10

"Enjoy being young while it lasts, 'cause in the blink of an eye you'll be all grown up."

Madison, Age 11

"You don't live forever, so cherish every moment even if it's bad."

Emory, Age 11

"Enjoy the easy life while you can. It won't last forever."

Autumn, Age 14

"Don't take life and people for granted."

Mackenzie, Age 14

Living in the Moment

"Take time to breathe and care for yourself."

Destiny, Age 23
teacher

"Live your life as if every day is a new adventure."

Dustin, Age 38
healthcare administrator

"Don't put activities, adventures, and travel off; do some now. Associate with people you want to be like and understand that not everything is about you."

Ed, Age 61
librarian/clergy

"Some are old at 65, others are young at 95. My aim is to stay young at heart and enjoy each day."

Dot, Age 86

"Take one day at a time and enjoy your friends and family."

Clifton, Age 86
farmer

"Enjoy it (life) while it lasts."

Megan, Age 14

"Be grateful!!!! Nothing is promised to us in this life! I'm hoping you will have a profound moment when you realize that you must really <u>live</u> life!!! Life is so fragile, but we can't be afraid to live it. This means taking a risk when opportunity presents itself. To me, it's like hiking a trail. Sometimes it is so hard and so strenuous, you really think about turning around and going back. But you can't turn back --- you've got to see what's at the end of the trail. You may never have the opportunity to come back this way again and you would have missed all the beauty. To me, the saddest two words in the world are "what if?" Make it a point to live your life so that you won't look back with regret and have to say, "what if?"

Denise, Age 57
consultant

"Life is about relationships. No matter what age."

Cindy, Age 63

Relationships

WISDOM OF AGE

If you could share one thing about life (that you've learned so far) with someone younger than you, what would that advice be?

"Never mess with a girl that is sassy."

Jace, Age 7

"If they are having a baby (brother), it will be fun. Even though he may jump on you and throw trucks."

Chloe, Age 7

"Just because a friend tells you something, that doesn't mean it's true."

Solomon, Age 9

"No matter how bad your life gets, do not push the people who love you away."

Destiny, Age 13

"Friends come and go. Real friends stay."

Brianna, Age 14

"Choose your friends wisely."

Taylor, Age 15

Relationships

"Don't do drugs or alcohol or be a bully."

Justice, Age 10

"Don't go with the crowd. Be your own person."

Levi, Age 16

"Don't get pregnant before you're ready."

**Rachel, Age 19
college student**

"Get married before having children."

**Charity, Age 29
senior registered nurse's aide**

"Don't stay with your high school boyfriend when you go on to college. Freshman year is for exploring."

**Charla, Age 19
college student**

"While living at home, listen to the stories your guardians or parents tell you, remember all the details, and spend as much time as you can with your loved ones."

**Tara, Age 46
radio DJ**

WISDOM OF AGE

"Don't take someone for granted, because I thought my memaw was mean when I was young but I realized when I got older she loved me and really wanted to see me as much as she could. Love the people that will show you so much love."

Hunter, Age 14

"It is very important to get out there and meet people, even if you don't much feel like it. Other people and their stories are the spark that makes life worth living."

Andrea, Age 73
sociologist

"My advice to someone younger is to live, learn, and love. Live each day like you won't see tomorrow. Educate yourself. Learn something new; an instrument, a language, culture or education. No one can take this from you. Love. Try to love as much as you can. You don't have to understand them. It's not for you to understand, but you need these experiences. Some will hurt, but you will appreciate each relationship. The world needs more love."

Leslie, Age 31
hairstylist

"I don't know how to say her name but she is a hardworking woman and she just turned 90. I learned from her not to judge a book by its cover. My sister is younger. She is 8 and my advice to her is to enjoy life as a kid because it will change."

Dakota, Age 11

WISDOM OF AGE

"Keep an open mind as you grow older. Do not think you know everything. Welcome new experiences and new people, and learn to accept different opinions and ideas."

Michelle, Age 14

"Always listen to your parents." (They're always right even when you think they're wrong.)

Sydney, Age 17

"You can learn so much from every person who comes into your life. Don't just disregard a person because they may be the next person to change your life for the better; it always happens when you least expect it."

Sarina, Age 20
college student

"Relationships matter most. Invest time and energy in people for the best life experience."

Keith, Age 62
college professor

"If you want a friend, you have to be one yourself."

Nina, Age 90
retired teacher

Respect/Age

If you could share one thing about life (that you've learned so far) to someone younger than you, what would that advice be?

"One cannot be judged by age. Just as every 20-year-old is very different in intelligence, maturity, and judgement, so is everyone at <u>every</u> age."

Ginger, Age 80
retired school psychologist/counselor

"Enjoy your youth; it goes by much faster as you age."

Phillip, Age 78

"Being active, involved, positive, caring about our world and in charge of yourself is what keeps us feeling young."

Paula, Age 65
registered nurse

"Everybody is unique so you should just be yourself."

Harlee, Age 11

"Do not judge anyone by what they look like on the outside."

Hannah, Age 9

Respect/Age

"Do not judge people by how old they are and the effects of aging about them. It only matters on how they act on the inside."

Kadan, Age 11

"Older people have more wisdom than we do."

Carley, Age 12

"Listen to the person older than you. This would be my younger sister because she thinks she is the oldest and there are lots of people in the world that are older than her."

Isaac, Age 12

"You can always learn from others no matter how old they are."

Cecilia, Age 14

"Old people have many common characteristics (deteriorating health, etc.), but retain their distinct personalities and should be regarded as individuals."

**Nancy, Age 82
retired teacher**

"Just because they are in their 20's or older than you, does not mean they are old."

Carley, Age 12

"Don't spend your life being someone you're not."

Maeleigh, Age 10

"I would tell them to be themselves and follow their dreams and don't let people tell you anything else."

Dylan, Age 12

"Don't let people put you down just by the words they say."

Liliana, Age 10

"Be yourself. It's better to like who you truly are than to fake it to please other people. So, paint if that's what you like or don't be afraid to rock that new hairstyle, because everything works out in the end."

Hailey, Age 13 (almost 14)

"Don't listen to what other people say about you and just be yourself because that's how God created you and you should love yourself for (who) you are and not about what others want you to be."

Olivia, Age 11

"Be confident in yourself. A lot of times I've worried over tests, but when you are ready and sure of yourself you are already a step ahead of the game."

Melisa, Age 14

"To really be confident you have to figure out what makes you, you. Surround yourself with people who love you, and friends that aren't fake."

Ashton, Age 15

"Never change who you are to fit in. Surround yourself with people that love you, and friends that aren't fake."

Catherine, Age 16

Encouragement

"Just because of your age doesn't mean you can't make a change in the world."

Sophia, Age 9

WISDOM OF AGE

If you could share one thing about life (that you've learned so far) with someone younger than you, what would that advice be?

"Try your hardest and do your best."

Aubrey, Age 7

"Life gets hard but you will get through it. You will make new friends and create a new chapter of life!"

😊 *Kayleigh, Age 9*

"Don't give up at something you are good at."

Jayden, Age 10

"Just keep going with what life throws at you."

Tory, Age 10

"Always be yourself."

Brianna, Age 10

"Don't let anyone disrespect you."

Cade, Age 10

"Follow your dreams and not someone else's."

Tayrn, Age 9

WISDOM OF AGE

""Don't be afraid to pursue what makes you happy. Do not let anyone else around you deter you from doing what you love. Don't worry about what others may think. If what you are pursuing is healthy and makes you happy, it is the right path."

Michael, Age 28
special education teacher

"Life is about following your passion . . .in your life, your love, your work. Try not to worry about failing, or what other people think."

Jack, Age 57
CEO, tech company for older adults

"Life is too short to not follow your dreams; set goals, and spend time doing what you enjoy. Don't take yourself too seriously. Find something to be encouraged by or to laugh at in every situation."

Dorothy, Age 68
legal assistant

Perceptions, Realities and Numbers

In the Foreword to this book, I pointed out the importance of putting the term "old" into perspective. I shared that while there is no set definition or general agreement on the age at which a person is considered old, the fact remains that our society has made a concerted effort over the years to quantify it.

Various ages continue to be used to determine things like retirement, eligibility for federal and state government benefit programs, Social Security, employee pensions, healthcare, home health, public amenities, "senior" discounts and so much more.

It's part of the lexicon of certain shopping days, "early bird" specials, and movie discounts. Age is used to identify housing preferences, buying habits, where certain people live, how they live, their voting habits, relative worth, physical and mental acuities. It is also used to presume an elder parent, grandparent, client, customer, or patient's interests and needs without ever asking them.

With all the attention being placed on the elderly, why is it that so few of us see ourselves as part of that elusive number we are attempting to reach, serve, or influence?

Over the years, I've given quite a few talks on the topic of aging. Usually it's to a room full of people "of a certain age." I'll usually start my conversation by asking, "Are there any old people in the room?" As you can imagine, very few hands go up. I'll then ask how many of them know someone who is "old." At that point, pretty much every hand goes up! It would appear, that we may not be aging ourselves, however, we're almost certain we can spot the ones who are.

This aversion to being thought of as "old," yet knowing that there are "old" people out there, made me think. What if I asked a random group of people if they would tell me at what age they thought a person might be considered old?

Some 500 people, ages five to 103, gave me their responses. The results can be found in the survey that follows and the observations that go along with it. You are free to draw your own conclusions.

The findings were derived using the responses of school-aged children from kindergarten through grade 12, and a select number of adults. For purposes of this study, adults were separated into two groups: adults, age 21 to 64, and retirees. Retirees were defined as age 65 and older, whether they were or were not retired.

Due to the qualitative nature of this study and because children were purposely over-sampled, children make up 75 percent of the sample, while the two adult groups are about evenly split between adults and retirees. This was done to see how each group might view being "old."

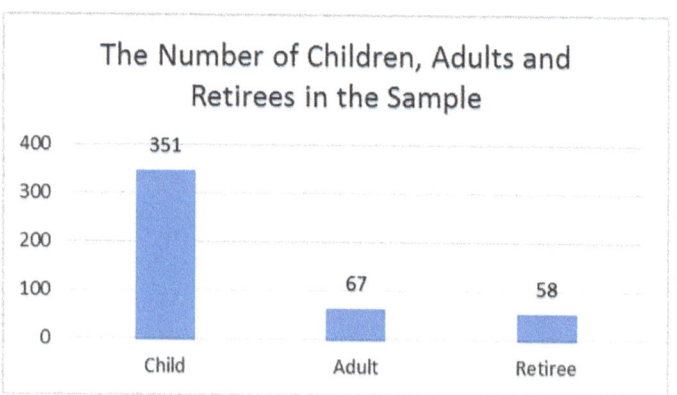

As you can see from the following graph, well over 80 percent of each group knows someone who is old.

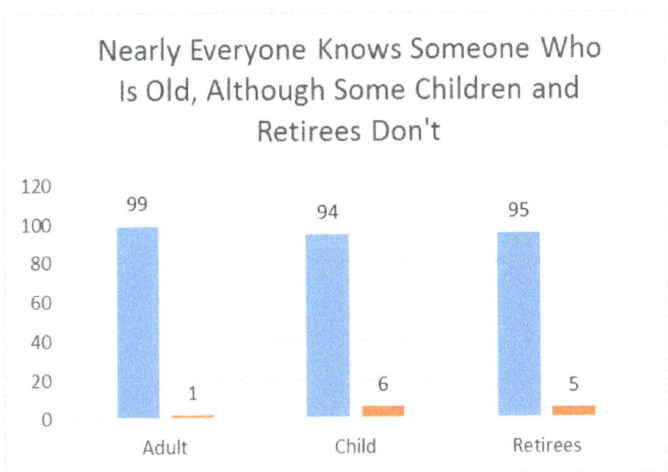

Children, on average, think someone is old at 70, while adults think someone is old on average at 78. Those who could retire, the retirees, think someone is old on average at 89.

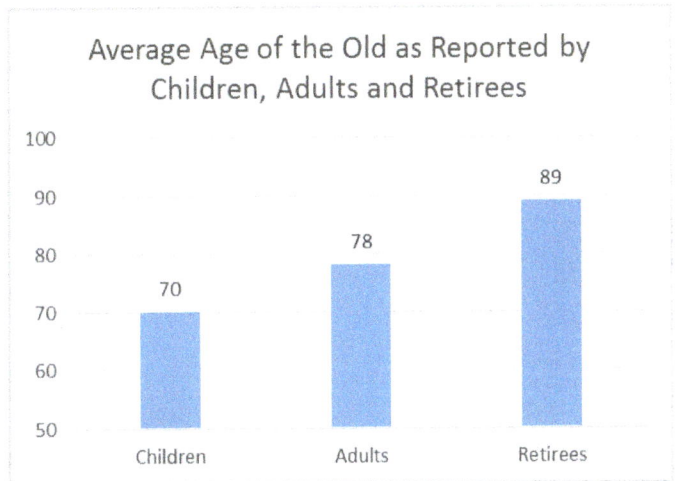

It would appear from these findings that the perception of old is very much related to the age of the person defining "old." Even among children, who define "old" as considerably younger than the other two groups, old is on average defined as a full five years later than the age we tend to think of as retirement age.

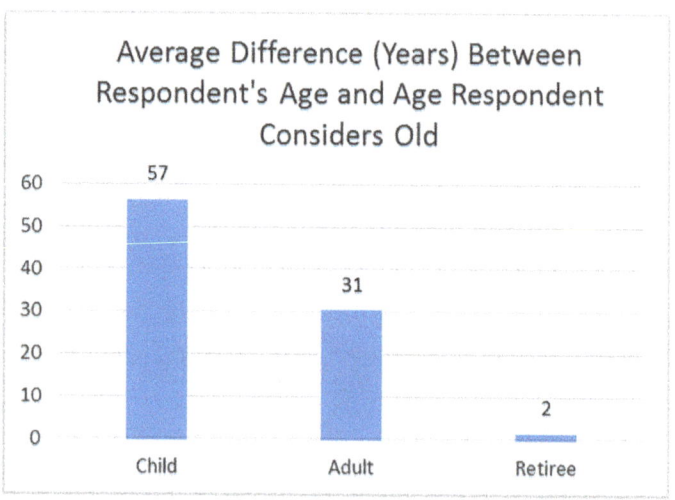

It is also worth noting the disparity among age groups in determining the average age range of a person they consider old.

Respondents in the study were also asked *"If you could share one thing about life (that you've learned so far) to someone younger than you, what would that advice be?"* Responses were coded and a brief analysis of their comments are presented here.

A respondent could give more than one response to the question, so the percentages given are the percentages of all responses, not all respondents.

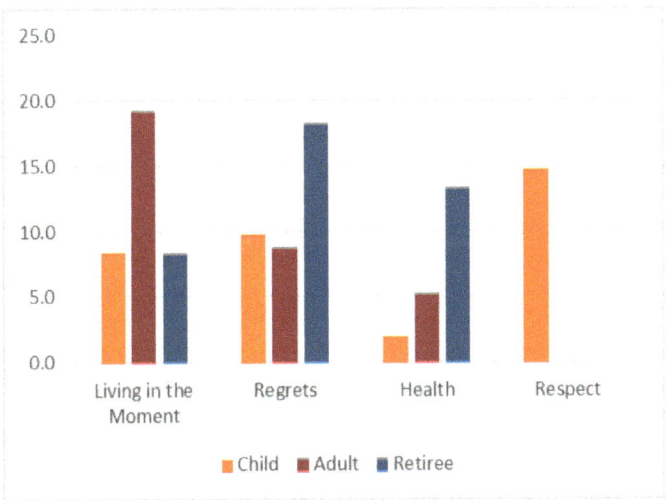

The most frequent response categories among all respondents included acceptance/faith, hindsight and encouragement. However, the responses were not the same for children, adults and retirees.

Adults were more likely to respond with a comment that suggested living in the moment, while retirees were more likely to note regrets and health. Children were more likely to respond with comments related to respect.

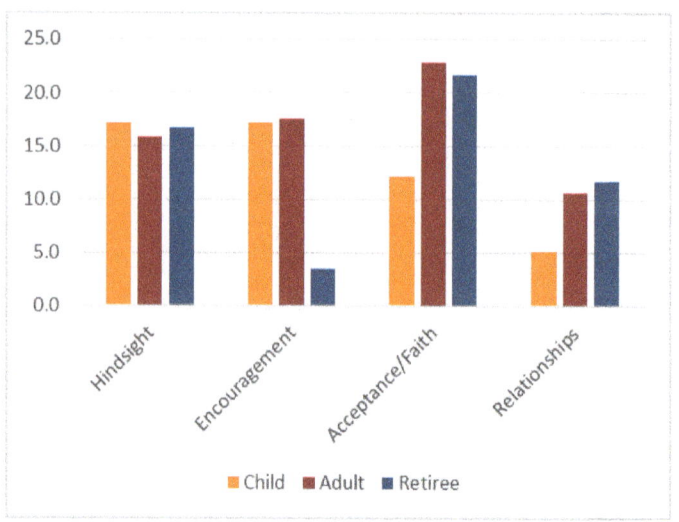

Still, children, adults and retirees were quite similar on some of their responses. All three groups were equally likely to mention hindsight. Children and adults were about equally likely to mention encouragement and acceptance/faith, while adults and retirees were just as likely to mention relationships.

At what age do you think a person should be considered old?

"Depends on the individual we are referring to. Generally speaking, I would say 85, but someone who is 50 can act "old" and I would happily give them that label."

Shirley, Age 95

"In their 80's." **Hannah, Age 94**

"50." **Ada, Age 93**

"90." **Irene, Age 93**

"65." **Keith, Age 92**

"92." **Judith, Age 91**

"When he/she can no longer live independently or presents a danger to themselves or others."

Marguerite, Age 89

"Age is just a number, it's how healthy you are that matters." **Betty, Age 88**

"It's your frame of mind. Some are old at 65 others are young at 95." **Dot, Age 86**

"70." *Melvin, Age 70*

"70." *Wanda, Age 80*

"It depends on the person. Some are "old" before 60. Some are "young" at 90."

Ginger, Age 80

"The number is unimportant; the person's ability AND DESIRE to participate in life determines if they have reached "old.""

Janet, Age 73

"Age is more a frame of mind than a chronological year." *Garth, Age 74*

"Depending on the way they act I'd say 90."

Joan, Age 73

"Too subjective. Can be at 60 if ill, not old at 90 if functional. That being said, probably late 70's."

Harriette, Age 70

"Old age is a state of mind. It is attitude! You can be old at any age; it is just a number."

Sharon, Age 71

"That's not my business."

Stella, Age 70 something

"Never if they are young at heart."   **Nancy, Age 69**

"I don't often use that word. The closest is "older." "Old" to me means worn out, used up, or historic, antiquated. "Older" means having lived longer, having more life experience, having a larger perspective, sometimes having greater maturity."

Theresa, Age 71

"60."   **Mary, Age 92 ½**

"When one's abilities are not sufficient."

Stanley, Age 92

"92."   **Judith, Age 91**

"As old as me."   **Hugh, Age 90**

"When they aren't physically able to do as they have in the past."

Ophelia, Age 83

"Is there an age?"   **Sandy, Age 83**

"81." *Dolly, Age 80*

"100." *Ann, Age 80*

"When they think they are old."

Sally, Age 82

"Even though I work in a field entirely connected to aging, I don't think in aging terms. I seem to resist broad generalizations, about age, about gender, about just anything. I really prefer to look at people as whole, whether they are 3 years old or 90 years old."

Katherine, Age 66

"When you lose your desire to laugh and enjoy life."

Ellen, Age 79

"80." *Joel, Age 73*

"100." *Janet, Age 74*

"When they are unable to care for themselves."

Sharon, Age 71

"When they feel it." Over 70.

Frank, Age 70

Perceptions, Realities and Numbers

"Never –It's not a matter of age, but perspective."
Ruth, Age 68

"I don't think age is the determining factor in being "old." I think attitude is the most important thing. Even when you can't do much or are slow in doing things, you might still be a contributor to the community."
Dorothy, Age 68

☺ "Much older than I am. 85 plus."
Magdalena, Age 66 and ½

"Whenever they act 'old.'"
Edwin and Sylvia, Ages 83 and 80

"100." **Sylvia, Age 66**

"Mom will soon be 97. That's old." **Frank, Age 65**

"77." **Alan, Age 65**

"Really doesn't correlate to age." **Paula, Age 65**

"When they start saying phrases such as "only the good die young."
Charles, Age 64

WISDOM OF AGE

"100 Plus." *Gil, Age 64*

"85." *Alex, Age 63*

"70." *Gladys, Age 63*

"75." *Tim, Age 63*

"Dead – ha! Functional status > Chronological Age, but if we must, 80." *Keith, Age 62*

"Never." *Gary, Age 62*

"No arbitrary age: I have learned that age is an attitude; not a simple number or birth date."

Robert, Age 61

"Older than me." *Ed, Age 61*

"The day they stop taking interest in new ideas."

Peter, Age 61

"50" *DG, Age 61*

"90." *Gail, Age 61*

"80 Plus." *Vickie, Age 58*

Perceptions, Realities and Numbers

"Can't put a number on it, it's all relative. My sister is "old" and she's 60. My other sister is 72 and she's not old." **Jack, Age 57**

"Depends on the person and circumstance. I know "old" 60-year-olds and "young" 90-year-olds. I am younger at 56 than I was at 46 given life changes." **Marc, Age 56**

"I think this totally depends on the person. Some people act far too old well before their years, and some seem to keep a vibrant and younger outlook on life in general well into their seventies and mid-eighties." **Mike, Age 49**

"80." **Vernon, Age 47**

"90." **Tonya, Age 47**

☺ "Not sure. In this day and age, even centenarians seem youthful." **Angel, Age 47**

"When they are afraid to hit the gas pedal while out driving." **Tara, Age 46**

WISDOM OF AGE

"People should start being considered old when they start acting like it to a degree. I have seen people in their 20's act "old"."
Thomas, Age 44

"90."
Louise, Age 43

"80."
Jackie, Age 42

"60."
Ki-Hwan, Age 60

"70."
Dustin, Age 38

"80."
Jennifer, Age 33

"Rather than an arbitrary number, I believe "old" happens when one stops setting goals and looking forward to pursuing them, and when one is only able to find satisfaction by living in the past."
Lorne, Age 34

"Never (That would just be rude). LOL."
Stephen, Age 32

"I think it depends on how they feel--there is no set number. The "youngest" person I know, meaning they report they feel old' is 56."
Beth, Age 34

"70."
Jonathan, Age 29

"100." **Charity, Age 29**

"When you "feel" old "You're old." **Raynikkia, Age 22**

"70 Plus." **Aaron, Age 21**

"65." **Tyler, Age 21**

"Dead . . . Or maybe 70." **Alexys, Age 21**

"Never, because the word "old" has so many negative connotations. There are people I know who have lived many years but their attitudes are so positive and they are in good physical/mental shape. Then there are others I know in their 70's who themselves say they "feel old" because they have physical disabilities. I think we need a better term to describe what we are saying. It's a matter of perspective. Young children think their parents are old, but when you are in your thirties, you might think someone in their 80's is old and realize how young 30 felt. Also, people throw away "old things." They get rid of them and replace them with something new. Sometimes "old things" are good, like vintage items that have now come back in style. Who decides what to get rid of and what to bring back? Who places importance on these things? Who sets the tone for this? Can we set a more positive tone for what "old" means and define it?"

April, Age 38

WISDOM OF AGE

"80." *Sara, Age 20*

"*Physically: whenever they cannot do all they want to be able to do. Mentally: never.*" *Sarina, Age 20*

"75." *Rachel, Age 19*

"50." *Roslyn, Age 19*

"110." *Landon, Age 10*

"100." *Jonah, Age 5*

"*My mommy is pretty old.*" *Jaxon, Age 5*

"100." *Bryce, Age 12*

"100." *Abigail, Age 6*

"99." *Aubrey, Age 7*

"99." *Jacob, Age 18*

"90." *Hannah, Age Nine ½*

"90." *Connor, 14 years old*

"79." *Braden, Age 8*

"73." *Keaton, 8 and a half*

"Man 70's; Woman – late 80's."	*Evan, Age 12*
"Late 70's and up."	*Sydney, Age 17*
"69."	*Jackson, Age 6*
"65."	*Carson, Age Nine*
"65."	*Joseph, Age 13*
"65."	*Kaelyn, Age 17*
"61."	*Lilly, Age 6*
"60."	*Aiden, Age 11*
"60."	*Tanner, Age 17*
"60-70."	*Hailey, Age 13 almost 14*
"59."	*Colton, Age 9*
"59."	*Kayden, Age 10*
"55."	*Abby, Age 16*
"50."	*Genisis, Age 10.5*
"49."	*Ashley, Age 8*
"47."	*Jace, Age 7*

WISDOM OF AGE

"45."   *Toby, Age 10*

"45."   *Josh, Age 14*

"41."   *Joshua, Age 10*

"40."   *Addison, Age 10*

"39."   *Mason, Age 9*

"35."   *Jimmy, Age 14*

"33."   *Felipe, Age 7*

"32."   *Clayton, Age 15*

"30."   *Levi, Age 9*

"29."   *Trenton, Age 7*

"26."   *Skye, Age 5*

"22."   *Katie, Age 5*

"21."   *Nate, Age 11*

"20."   *Rachel, Age 10*

"18."   *Anna, 11 years old*

"18 and older."   *Levi, 9 years old*

"17."	*Caleb, Age 9*
"16."	*Aiden, Age 5*
"14."	*Juantele, Age 6*
"11."	*Jayden, Age 5*
"10."	*Jakayla, Age 5*
"9."	*Omar, Age 5*

As you have seen throughout this book, no one can quite agree on when someone should be considered "old" or even if a number should be applied. Some see it as an attitude; others as a matter of physical or mental decline. Still others see it as a time in one's life when they stop looking forward or simply stop questioning, "why?"

If a common definition cannot be found, then the question we should be asking ourselves is why our society puts so much emphasis on age? Or, more precisely, why is there "Ageism"? The World Health Organization sees ageism as universal, citing Belgium, England, France, Spain, and Sweden as just some examples of other countries where age discrimination persists.

While ageism is predominantly used in relationship to the treatment of older people, the term is meant to describe stereotyping and discriminating against any individual or group based solely on their age. It would apply equally therefore, if we were to ignore the ideas of someone because they are considered "too young" or presume someone should behave a certain way simply because they are considered "old".

Different dictionaries have ascribed different meanings to the term "ageism." One cites it as "unfair treatment of a person or group based on prejudice." Another describes it as "a tendency to regard older persons as debilitated, unworthy of attention, or unsuitable for employment."

Stereotypes are often based on a "grain of truth." However, they can often cause harm when the content of the stereotype is incorrect or so strongly held that it overrides evidence to the contrary for most individuals or members of that group. In the workplace, that could mean stereotyping older workers as being resistant to change, not creative, cautious, slow to make judgments, lower in physical capacity, uninterested in technological change, and difficult to train. It could also mean ignoring a child or teenager's comments and ideas simply because they lack "experience" or are expected to be "seen and not heard".

Because ageism is so ingrained it may be even harder to eliminate than other forms of stereotyping. There is evidence of this in movies, on TV, in advertising, and in life. It's in the images we see and the phrases we hear growing up and what we continue to take for granted growing older.

How many times have you heard or used phrases like "senior moment", "dirty old man", "second childhood", "past their prime", or similar metaphors to describe someone without considering the significance of these statements?

The use of stereotyping and patronizing language, whether toward the elderly or the young, has been shown to affect peoples' self-esteem and behaviors. After repeatedly hearing a stereotype that older or younger people are useless, they may begin to feel like dependent, non-contributing members of society. They may start to perceive themselves in the same ways that others in society see them. They may also, based upon a lifetime of exposure, engage in self-stereotypes, directing what they've heard inward to describe themselves ("when you get to be my age . . ."). Such behavior reinforces the present stereotypes and perpetuates what amounts to a self-fulfilling prophecy.

In considering that prophecy, I thought it would be helpful to bring your attention to two quotes. One expresses the definition of old age as something perpetually in the future and therefore unattainable (and undesirable); and the other speaks in terms of attitude and how we live the years that we have.

"Old age is always fifteen years older than I am."

Oliver Wendell Holmes Jr.
Supreme Court Justice
1841-1935, Age 93

"It is not the years in your life but the life in your years that counts."

Adlai E. Stevenson II
U.S. Senator, lawyer, Diplomat
1900-1965, Age 65

Whether we choose to deny it, look forward to it, or make the most of the time we have, the fact remains that many of you reading this, barring any major conflict, plague, or incurable disease, can expect to live even longer.

In 2012, the United Nations estimated that there were 316,600 centenarians (age 100 or more) worldwide, while the number of centenarians living in the U.S. stood at approximately 54,000. Today, due to many factors that contribute to life expectancy, people 85 and over are now the fastest growing age group percentage-wise. And, according to the Office for National Statistics in England, one-third of all babies born today are expected to live to be 100.

There are many factors contributing to this longevity revolution. They range from heredity and nutrition to advances in medicine, medical treatment, and quality of life. It further includes how we choose to envision the lives that we lead.

The general consensus of available research conducted with centenarians points to the fact that they live with a sense of purpose, with a childlike curiosity about life, and with moderation in all things. Purpose and meaning are considered crucial to their health and long life.

This shift in demographics, along with what we are continuing to learn from these longevity pioneers, is forcing us to revisit outdated perceptions about age many have held for far too long. It is requiring us to rethink how we, and others, will live, work, grow up, and grow old in our communities, our nation, and the world around us.

In thinking through that question, consider too, that the most abundant resource we have at our disposal is human capital. Then ask yourself why, in these times of uncertainty, do we continue to marginalize the very

People whose own sense of wisdom, perspective, and view of life may contribute to the very answers we seek.

It's the difference between being empowered or powerless. Empowerment begins when we ask what the other person thinks. Change is what happens when we put their thoughts into action.

To eliminate ageism, we must change the culture. That can only come about in how we see, treat, and engage one another. It starts with the very young and continues with the very old and comes about when we seek out the Wisdom of Age.

Postscript

This book is just a first step in beginning the conversation about ageism. There is much more that each of us can do. I invite you to take the lead in your community by helping to promote more formal and informal conversation among your peers, classmates, or in your workplace.

Encourage intergenerational dialogue. Visit an elderly neighbor; take your child or encourage their teacher to take her class to a nursing home; start a program for children and adults to tutor or mentor one another. Gather life stories; encourage church, civic, and community leaders to get involved. Promote "age-friendly" communities.

Make it a point to share your experiences. There is so much more we each can say to and share with one another. I'm looking forward to continuing to listen and learn from people like you.

Visit me online, www.wisdomofage.net, fill out the survey, and let's continue to share what we've learned.

The Wisdom of Age Survey

Everyone ages, and with it comes wisdom to pass along to someone younger. Yours may have come from a family member or someone else you respected while growing up, or it may be lessons you've learned simply through living and experiencing life.

To learn what people of different ages and backgrounds think about age and wisdom, I'd like to invite you to take a few minutes to consider these few simple questions below, and submit your reply on our web site: www.wisdomofage.net.

What is your first name?

What is your age?

What is your current grade in school, or what is (or was) your occupation?

At what age do you think a person should be considered old?

If you can do anything you want to do with your life, now or in the future, what's one thing you can see yourself doing?

If you could share one thing about life that you've learned so far with someone younger than you, what would that advice be?

Some Very Special Responses

What is your first name? *Drexel*

How old are you? *100 years old*

What was your occupation? *Machinist for Boeing*

At what age do you think a person should be considered old? *75*

Do you know any "old" people? *"No, I don't."*

If you could share one thing about life (that you've learned so far) with someone younger than you, what would that advice be?

"Just enjoy life. Do as much as you can while you're able. I have always tried to travel as much as possible. I've gone on many trips across the globe. You get acquainted with a lot of people from many different walks of life when you travel."

Some Very Special Responses

What is your first name? *Elba*

How old are you? *100. I will be 101 in September.*

What was your occupation? *Dressmaker*

At what age do you think a person should be considered old? *90*

Do you know any "old" people? *"Yes, her."* (pointing to her friend.) If so, how old are they? *103*

If you could share one thing about life (that you've learned so far) with someone younger than you, what would that advice be?

"I can't believe I am 100 years old. Life has gone by so fast. I tried to be an honest and trusting person all of my life. Be thankful for what you have, laugh a lot, have a sense of humor. Respect and be kind to one another. Be responsible for yourself. Don't ask for handouts. Save your money for a rainy day!

Some Very Special Responses

What is your first name? *Genevieve*

How old are you? *103*

What was your occupation? *Credit Manager for three stores.*

At what age do you think a person should be considered old? *"I drove my car until I was 93. I don't know."*

Do you know any "old" people? *"A roomful."*

If so, how old are they? *"80's and 90's".*

If you could share one thing about life (that you've learned so far) to someone younger than you, what would that advice be?

"Make Jesus first!"

One Final Thought

Since we live in a world that would appear to value youth over age and success over failure, my advice to those younger than me is best expressed in an essay by Ralph Waldo Emerson, American essayist and poet (1803-1882). His advice then and my advice now would be:

"To laugh often and much; To win the respect of intelligent people and the affection of children; To earn the appreciation of honest critics and endure the betrayal of false friends; To appreciate beauty, to find the best in others; To leave the world a bit better, whether by a healthy child, a garden patch, or a redeemed social condition; To know even one life has breathed easier because you have lived. This is to have succeeded."

Jeff, Age 65
facilitator, conversationalist, and advocate
for living a life of passion and purpose

Special Thanks and Acknowledgement

No one goes through life on his or her own. It takes counsel, guidance, and support from family, friends, teachers, and others. Some enter our lives for a moment; others for a season; and still others for a lifetime. Each one teaches us something if we take the time to listen.

My thanks go out to everyone who has played a part in shaping my own life so far, as well as to all those who I can still expect to meet along the way.

The following individuals deserve special mention for the support they've given me in the writing of this book.

Elmer Thomas, Superintendent of Schools for Madison County, KY. Elmer understood that ageism demands a shift in cultural thinking, and to do that it must begin with our youth. Many of the wisdoms shared in this book came through his efforts and the support he received from the principals, teachers, and students, grades K through 12, in his district.

Vicki Short, Administrator, Berea Health and Rehabilitation Center *(Berea, KY) and* ***Gil Shew, Administrator, St. Andrews Continuum of Care Retirement Communities*** *(Richmond, KY).*

Vicki and Gil well know the rich and varied lives their residents have led and continue to lead. They recognize them as individuals and personalities, and treat them with the dignity and respect they deserve.

Jackie Burnside, Professor of Sociology, Berea College. Another believer in breaking down social stereotyping, Jackie was instrumental in getting several students and faculty to take part in the survey. Along with a sampling of other college students from around the country, she added much to the perspectives shared by young adults in this book.

Mark Greene, Digital Services Coordinator, Madison County Library, (Berea, KY.) Mark and many of the staff at the Madison County Library have been an invaluable resource in donating their time, talents, and technical expertise in helping to turn my ideas, research and concepts into a finished and accomplished book!

Tanya Stewart, artist and illustrator. Her whimsical eye, attention to detail, and flair for capturing the essence of our responders' thoughts added much to the look, feel, and theme of the project.

Andrea Carr, retired researcher, sociologist, consultant and contributor to this project. She, like so many others, serendipitously appeared when needed the most.

Dennis Tallon, Executive Coach & Leadership Development Professional. Dennis is a professional colleague, valued friend, and one of those special people whose support remains unequivocal and whose guidance and advice are greatly appreciated and reciprocated.

Denise Hagan Rubin, a wife, friend, confidant, professional colleague, and a personal cheerleader for encouraging the best in herself, others, and me. Her sense of fairness, trust, love, and concern for family, friends, and all creatures (large and small) is matched only by an ever-questioning curiosity about the world around her and the awe she finds in nature.

Sarina Bennette Rubin, a loving daughter, confidant, and honor student at the University of Oregon. Her journey to adulthood has been a source of joy, frustration, inspiration, and pride to me, her mother, Sharon, extended family and friends.

About the Author

Jeff Rubin is a civic improvement, community engagement, and communications professional who believes that every individual has the right to be heard and the power to make a difference regardless of their ability or age. He believes this to be especially true if there are decisions being made that impact the quality of any individual's life. A champion of inclusion and collaboration, he sees both as essential components in bringing about productive and effective change.

Jeff has been acknowledged for his efforts over the years, winning Editor and Publisher's top award for community service while marketing and directing several community newspapers, and later being recognized by his peers for leading and advancing older adult and intergenerational programs at the local, state, and national levels.

More recently, Jeff was appointed by the previous Kentucky Governor, Steve Beshear, to serve as a member of the Kentucky Institute on Aging, an advisory body to the Department of Aging and Independent Living. In addition, he hosts a radio talk show on contemporary community issues, and is a contributing columnist to print and online media.

Jeff has a daughter, Sarina, age 21, who attends college at the University of Oregon. He shares a consulting practice with his wife, Denise, in Berea, Kentucky where they live with their dog, Toby.

About the Illustrator

Kentucky native Tanya Stewart has been an illustrator for over 25 years. Her work appears in children's books, magazines, editorial cartoons, and greeting cards, as well as creating independent pieces and watercolor. She hopes to still be able to hike the Berea Pinnacles when she's 90.

www.ingramcontent.com/pod-product-compliance
Lightning Source LLC
Chambersburg PA
CBHW061233070526
44584CB00030B/4104